People at Work

Working for British Telecom

by Alison Sibley

*Photography by
Chris Fairclough*

Titles in the series

Working at an Airport
Working in the Army
Working for a Brewery
Working for British Telecom
Working on a Building Site
Working for a Bus Company
Working for a Chemicals Company
Working in the Civil Service
Working at a Coal Mine
Working in a Department Store
Working for an Electronics Company
Working on a Farm
Working for a Food Company
Working for a Garage
Working in a Hospital
Working in a Hotel
Working for an Insurance Company
Working at a Light Engineering Plant
Working on a Newspaper
Working for an Oil Company
Working for the Police Force
Working at a Port
Working for the Postal Service
Working in a Town Hall
Working for Yourself

Picture acknowledgement:
The photograph on p.6 is reproduced
by courtesy of the Post Office.

First published in 1984 by
Wayland (Publishers) Ltd
49 Lansdowne Place, Hove
East Sussex BN3 1HF, England

© Copyright 1984 Wayland (Publishers) Ltd

ISBN 0 85078 315 1

Phototypeset by Kalligraphics Ltd,
Redhill, Surrey
Printed and bound in Great Britain by
R. J. Acford Ltd, Industrial Estate, Chichester, Sussex

Contents

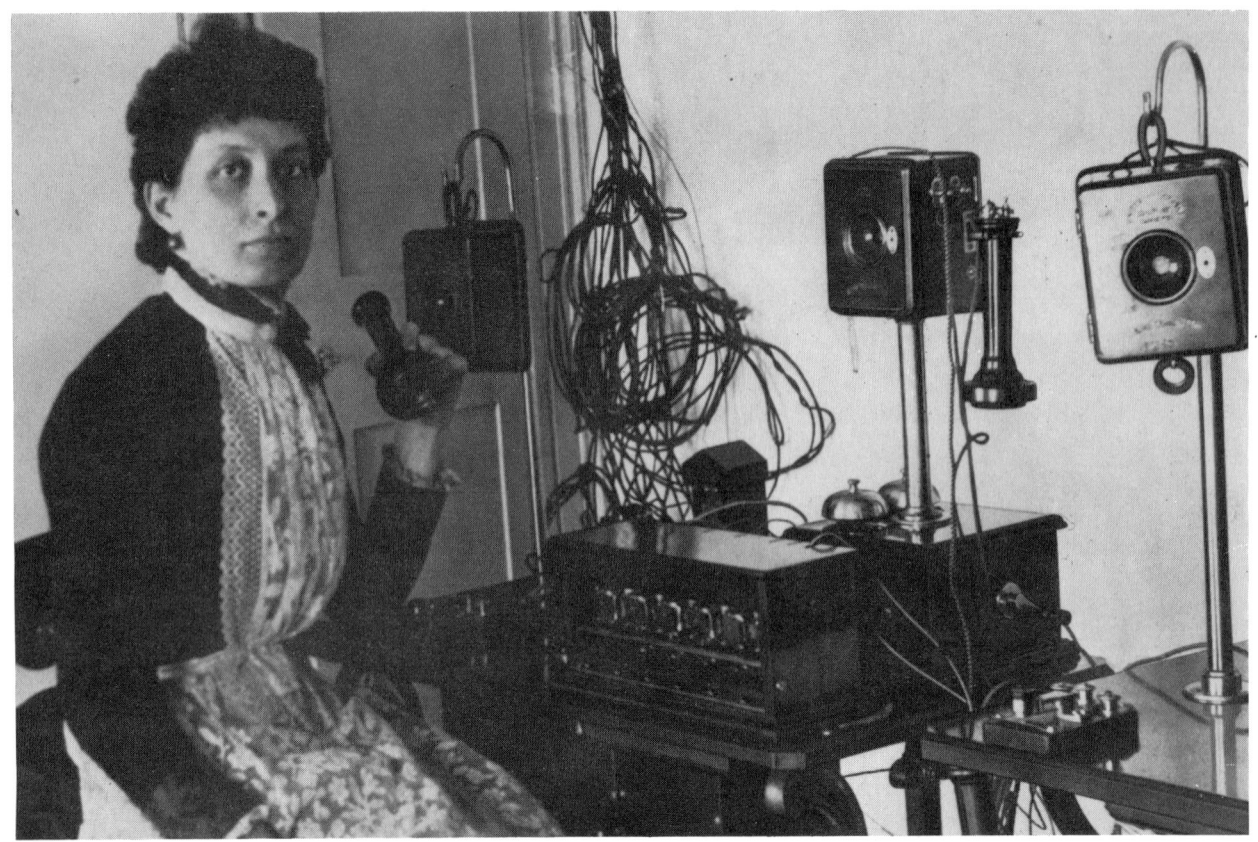

British Telecom and its history

The Croydon telephone exchange, 1884.

Telecommunications is one of the UK's biggest growth industries. We are living in a society which is hungry for information, and waiting for the next morning's newspaper to tell us the latest cricket score is no longer good enough. As the current communications revolution gathers momentum, British Telecom is keeping apace by installing equipment to extend international dialling and setting up electronic exchanges to give customers new facilities and better service.

Unlike some other technologies, the spread of telecommunications does not use up valuable land, pollute or threaten life, and so it is rarely impeded by objections from the public. The UK has one of the world's largest telecommunications systems, a network consisting not just of telephones, but telex, television and radio, computers, satellites, radiopaging, maritime services and a host of other facilities.

British Telecom employs almost a quarter of a million people in the UK with a wide variety of skills. There are over 300 motor transport workshops, and more than 55,000 vehicles currently covering around 300 million miles a year, making it the largest civilian fleet in western Europe. Every working day, about 3,500 catering staff provide thousands of meals at over 400 staff restaurants.

With annual sales approaching £6,000 million, almost 20 million exchange lines to maintain, and around 21,000 million calls to put through successfully each year, the size of British Telecom's operations would have astonished even the far-sighted Alexander Graham Bell, who invented the telephone in 1876.

Bell, who went to the universities of Edinburgh and London, specialised in the study of sound, and taught people who had defective speech or had been born deaf and therefore never learnt to speak. He emigrated to Canada when he was 23, and it was in Boston, Massachusetts, that he first succeeded in transmitting and receiving speech. The first telephones to be brought to this country were acquired by Sir William Preece, later engineer-in-chief of the Post Office.

The first telephone exchange in the UK, using Bell's patents, was opened at Coleman Street, London, in 1879. An American inventor, Thomas Alva Edison, also invented a telephone, and from 1880 onwards telephones were made combining the best aspects of both designs. The Post Office, which had been operating a telegraph system since 1870, eventually took over a number of private telephone companies which had started up, and opened a few exchanges of its own. From 1912, the telephone system became substantially unified and today, apart from Hull and the Channel Islands, British Telecom operates an entire national network.

The idea of connecting telephone lines by an automatic exchange is almost as old as the telephone itself, but the first person to develop a system suitable for large exchanges was Almon Strowger, of Kansas City, USA. Strowger's equipment was installed all over the UK, in small to fairly large towns. But there were special difficulties in very large towns and cities, such as London, until the Automatic Telephone Company of Liverpool developed a piece of equipment called a 'director' which enabled the Strowger exchange to be used in the very largest towns.

Sixty-two years after the first London to Paris call was manually connected, Queen Elizabeth made the first call by subscriber trunk dialling (STD) in 1958, from Bristol. Five years later followed international direct dialling (IDD). London and Manchester were the first two cities in the world to be able to dial their own inter-continental calls. A call to San Francisco, or Vancouver, may be carried in cable more than two miles deep in the Atlantic or go via a communications satellite over 20,000 miles above the surface of the earth. The most recent advances in technology are optical fibres, hair-thin strands of pure glass over which digital signals are transmitted by light pulses, and System X, a family of advanced digital switching systems designed for the 21st century.

Under the British Telecommunications Act of 1981, the telecommunications services provided by the Post Office were formed into a separate organization, and the new public corporation was called British Telecom. Private firms are now allowed to compete with British Telecom in many aspects of the telecommunications industry, and the 1984 Act established British Telecom as an independent business. Currently, nearly 60 million calls are made in the UK each day, and nearly 2,000 new telephones are installed every hour of the working day. Among the growing list of products and services British Telecom offers, are new ideas in communications like home banking and electronic mail.

British Telecom York

York Telephone Area employs nearly 1,800 people in a wide variety of jobs.

The twelve men and women featured in this book all work for British Telecom York, or York Telephone Area. At present the British Telecom network is subdivided into ten regions throughout the country, each under the control of a director and a regional board. These geographical regions are themselves split into areas, of which there are a total of 61 in the UK.

York Telephone Area is part of British Telecom's North Eastern Region, the headquarters of which are at Leeds. The area is run by a general manager, and an area board, consisting of heads of divisions. At one time the area offices were under the direct control of the regional headquarters (which in turn answers to Telecom Headquarters in London). But the general trend now is for each individual telephone area to be viewed as a profit-making organization in its own right.

There are plans for reorganization of the business, beginning in 1985. Both the number and geographical area of many British Telecom's units will be liable to change.

Although all the people in this book become aware now and again that they are working for a vast industry, and therefore enjoying all the benefits large companies enjoy, such as good wages, promotion prospects, training facilities, subsidized canteens, sports and social clubs and so on, they also feel that British Telecom is their very own business, which they are helping to make a success.

York Telephone Area covers around 2,500 square miles and its main offices are in the historic walled city of York, with its cathedral and castle. Altogether, the Area employs nearly 1,800 people, many working outside York in the 123 telephone exchanges and telephone engineering centres. The three largest categories of employees are engineering staff (numbering well over 1,000, including apprentices), telephonists and supervisors, and administrative and clerical staff. The rest of the employees are sales and traffic staff (traffic is the term used to refer to the volume of calls made through the telephone network) drawing office personnel, typists, catering staff, general assistants and cleaners.

Geographically large, York Telephone Area is mainly rural in character. Nevertheless, calls made by its telephone users in 1983 totalled 65.5 million. The Area made a total of £70 million in that year, over half coming from telephone calls alone.

All of which is far removed from the opening of the first National Telephone Company magneto exchange, which was situated over a chemist's shop in York, in 1886, with 11 subscribers making local calls for one penny a time. Six years later, the Post Office opened a rival magneto exchange and the NTC subscribers were provided with access to the Post Office trunk exchange which boasted just two lines between Lendal and Leeds. The Post Office bought out NTC in 1912 for around £12.5 million. The number of subscribers had by then reached 250. Now, York exchange serves nearly 31,000.

All the British Telecom staff in this book joined the company with the hope of a good career ahead, whether they started with only a few qualifications or whether they had a university degree. But in view of changing times, more than one pointed out the need for further qualifications after 'O' levels. It is still possible to work your way up from starting as a a sixteen-year-old school-leaver, and full training facilities are available. However, British Telecom needs to keep in the forefront of world technology and needs to employ young men and women with degrees in engineering, computing, finance and accounting subjects, to help manage one of the largest telecommunications networks in the world.

At the British Telecom headquarters in York, there is a 'business centre', where customers can try out new telephone systems for themselves.

Eric Deighton
Technical officer in training

Eric Deighton is 30 years old and came to British Telecom after being a mechanical engineer with the RAF and British Rail. He installs large switchboards in offices and factories, some with as many as 150 telephone extensions. He plans to study to keep up with new developments in technology.

In my job, as a technical officer in training, interesting things are always happening. I fit the larger sort of switchboards in offices and factories, the sort with up to 20 exchange lines and between 80 and 150 telephone extensions. The day when I am replacing a customer's old switchboard with a 'new one, or extending his old one, is called a 'changeover' day. I've got the time it takes between disconnecting the old and bringing the new switchboard into service down to a fine art. In fact, down to about ten minutes. However, there's a lot of planning involved before hand.

In a place such as a hospital, the length of time the building is without telephones is very important. One changeover day, a Saturday, I had to go to a hospital on the coast, about 40 miles from the York Area office, which is my base. I travel all over the York Telephone Area in my own van, spending around three weeks to a month on each job. Anyway, on this particular changeover day, myself and another fitter had installed 60 telephones by 3 o'clock in the afternoon, only to find that every one was faulty (a manufacturer's fault). So we sent someone at the speed of knots back to York, a round trip of 80 miles, to pick up 60 new telephones. When he got back, we fitted those, only to find that they were faulty as well! So it was back to York for yet another batch – and we finally got the switchboard working at 7 o'clock at night. Despite all this, at no time was the hospital cut off, because we rigged a temporary emergency service for them.

Excitement like that doesn't happen every day of course, but it does from time to time, and it's part of the reason why I enjoy my work. This is the best job I've ever had, but I didn't walk straight into it.

I left school in 1968 when I was 16, with seven CSE passes in technical drawing, geo-

Eric discusses the day's job with his boss.

graphy, English, woodwork, metalwork, maths and physics. My first job was as an apprentice mechanical engineer for a firm which eventually went bankrupt, and so I was made redundant. I'd always lived in Yorkshire, but when I joined the air force I had to move to RAF Cranwell, in Lincolnshire, where I worked for three years as an aircraft mechanic. We parted company on the best of terms and I went to work for British Rail at their engineering works back here in York.

The job at British Telecom wasn't advertised, but I had been thinking about a change for a long while, as I wanted something more technically advanced than what I was doing at British Rail. So I wrote a letter giving details of my previous jobs, and was put on a waiting list and eventually got called for an interview.

That was seven years ago now, and after passing the interview I had a thorough medical. I was engaged as an installer, who is someone who goes around and fits telephones in private houses. My engineering background proved an advantage and I came into British Telecom as a technician IIB,(a rank just below a technician IIA). Once you've been out by yourself for about three months you are considered competent enough and you are classed a technician IIA. I had been installing telephones in houses for about six months when I was asked to go on fitting duties.

Whatever your job entails, British Telecom will teach you how to do it, but as there are no training facilities here in York, I had to go away on courses. I did my basic training in Otley, in Yorkshire, and every so often I would find I was off on another course. For instance, before you can go up a telephone pole, you have to do a training course on cable work, for safety reasons.

As a fitter, I dealt with small telephone systems for business customers, such as switchboards, call-connect systems and so on: all a bit more complicated than installing residential 'phones. I went on several more courses to learn how to be a fitter and after three years I moved on to customer works group, still here in York, and now I'm fitting even bigger systems. As yet I have no staff under me and my supervisor is a technical officer, which is what I'm training to be. As I usually travel around on my own, I have a lot of control over my own work, and I like that aspect of the job.

Before setting off, Eric loads his van outside the engineering stores and checks that he has everything he needs.

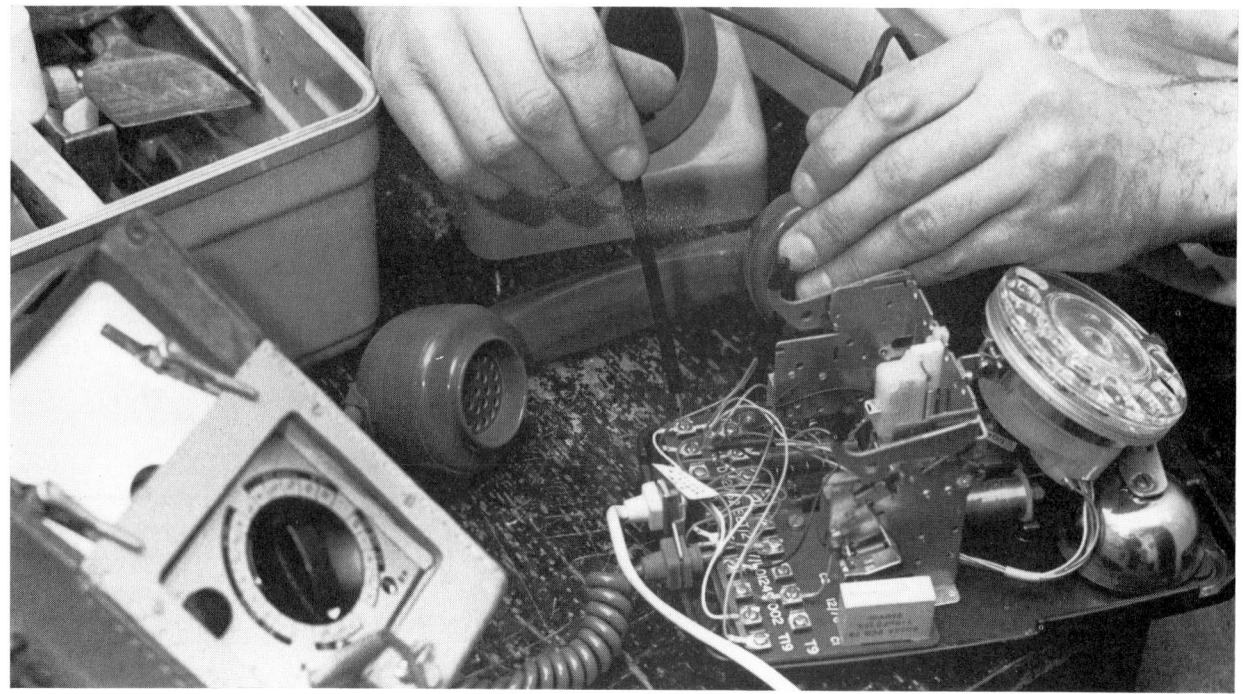

The inside of a telephone is no mystery to Eric.

Sometimes if I'm working out of York I'll have my van at home with me in the morning in Huntingdon, which is three miles from York. When I'm starting from home I always ring into the office either to let them know where I'm going to be, or to find out what job I have to do that day.

I work a seven and a half hour day, starting at 8.15 a.m. Once at the customer's premises, I get straight down to sorting out the job in hand, breaking for an hour for lunch. At the moment I'm fitting a Monarch switchboard which has 120 exchange lines and I'm starting from scratch, which means I have to do all the cabling out of the building as well. This will take about three weeks. If the customer already has a switchboard, all I have to do is fit another one in, as the cabling may be there already, or only need adding to. I don't have to show the customer how to work the switchboard, as two instructors from British Telecom go out to train him when the system is fitted and working.

One very interesting job I had was setting up the business centre at the York Telephone Area headquarters. This is a room where the public can come in and actually try out various sorts of working telephones, and different

Nearly 2,000 new telephones are installed every hour of the working day.

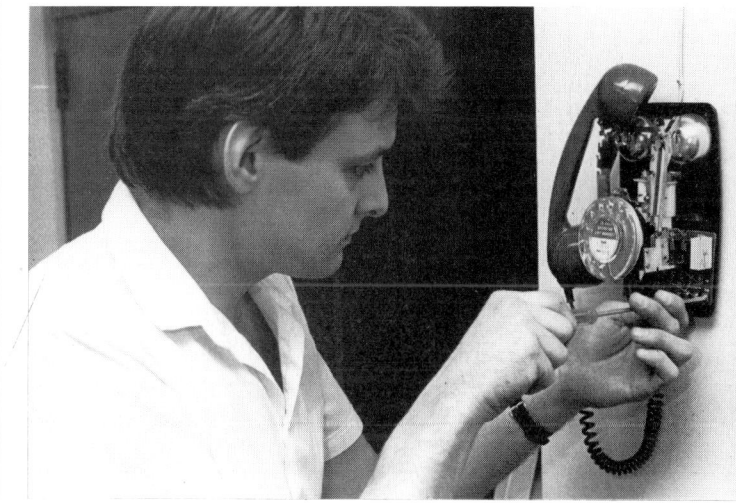

kinds of switchboards with numerous functions. I put most of those systems in myself.

I've no current plans for after I've become a technical officer, because it will be quite a long time before I'm eligible for the next step of promotion. It took me five years on a day-release scheme and at evening classes at technical college to get my Technician Education Council Certificate (TEC), levels 1 to 3, which are the necessary qualifications to become a technical officer. I was very much encouraged to study by British Telecom and I took them up on it. I shall carry on studying, as there are other things I want to do, such as courses on microprocessing systems, because I feel it is really important to keep up with new technology.

Up to a year ago my spare time was taken up with studying, but now, when I'm not helping with my three children or taking them out, I play badminton, do a bit of running and I also read quite a lot. Last year I managed to take the family to Greece for a holiday, but we don't usually go abroad. The pay is

The rack is now in place, so all the colour-coded wires need sorting out.

A delicate touch is needed here – faulty wires could lead to complaints from a disgruntled customer or even prove dangerous.

very reasonable compared with other companies in the area. We run a car and we've bought our own house which has stretched our finances a bit, but I will get more money as a technical officer, which is quite a good rank to have achieved in British Telecom.

Paul Warnock
Telephone pole erector

Paul Warnock was looking for job security when he applied to British Telecom, after having been made redundant twice as a mechanic. He works on one of the two pole-erecting teams in York Area. He enjoys the varied nature of his work, as well as being able to work outside.

I was crazy about cars when I was a kid. I was more interested in what went on under the bonnet of a car than in the world outside! I had always wanted to work in the motor trade, so when I left school, I set out to become a mechanic. It wasn't until several years later, after I'd been made redundant as a mechanic twice – with a wife and three young children to feed – that I started thinking about getting a more steady, secure job and applying to British Telecom. Fortunately, I had passed my Heavy Goods Vehicle (HGV) driving test while I was a mechanic, and this helped me get the pole-erecting job which involves driving a very heavy lorry, loaded with telephone poles. I've always been mechanically-minded, so I was glad to find a job where I could still work with heavy machinery and tools, and I love working out of doors, even in the winter.

I went to a secondary school in Manchester, where my family lived, and we moved to York after I'd left school at 16, with no qualifications at all. Once in York, I got an apprenticeship with a garage and during that time I did a City and Guilds course in vehicle crafts studies, and later qualified as a motor mechanic. It was also while working for this garage that I got my HGV Grade III licence. As I'd always wanted to be a mechanic, everything seemed to be going according to plan, but after two years I was made redundant. I transferred to the Department of the Environment, and was a mechanic in their workshops for the next three years, before being made redundant yet again. By this time I was really beginning to feel that I was in the wrong trade for job security, and although I went to work for another car dealer in York fairly soon afterwards, I started thinking about a career with a more promising future.

A friend of mine had worked for British Telecom down in Manchester, and this gave me the idea of writing to British Telecom here in York, setting out my career to date and asking about any vacancies they might have. No sooner had I done that, than I saw an advert in the local jobcentre for someone to join one of British Telecom's pole-erecting teams, so I made an official application as well. Within a couple of weeks I went along for an interview and did a series of little tests, including how to wire an electric plug, and saying why the wires were colour-coded and so on. The three men on the panel made particular reference to my HGV licence; to the fact that I'd not been sacked from my previous jobs but made redundant; and that I was

Above *Paul and his workmate prepare to remove the old pole.*

Below *Paul sets up the road signs to warn motorists of the work ahead.*

obviously mechanically-minded. On my side, I made a point of saying I was looking for a steady job as I was married with three children. I also had a medical, and about six to eight weeks later was accepted for the job.

I started in June 1980, when I was 25. The first few weeks were incredibly hectic. Everyone who joins British Telecom spends some time in each department, and although I'd applied for the pole-erecting job, I also spent about a week or so with a jointing team (these are the men who go underground and put jointing boxes on the cables) and then another week with an overhead crew, learning about wiring between poles. I went to the training school at Otley, where I advanced quite quickly to the pole-erecting course, which was held at Bletchley. I'm not studying for any more qualifications at the moment, although British Telecom does encourage you to do extra courses. Mind you, I have recently applied to become a fitter in the installation department. The trouble is, these are the prime jobs so they're hard to get.

For the moment, I'm in one of the two pole-erecting teams here in York. There are two men in each team, a driver and an assistant, and I'm the assistant on this team. We both do exactly the same job, except the driver gets paid a little bit more and has usually been with British Telecom longer. My take home pay is £142. I can do a limited amount of overtime and I get an allowance of £1.30 a day for a meal. Our job is to take down and erect telephone poles which carry overhead cables.

Ladder rungs and a steel crosspiece have to be attached to the new pole before it is erected.

Each morning we report to York depot at 8.00 a.m., sign-on, then ring up the control office to find out where we have to go that day. Then we go to the stores, pick up some poles – not literally of course, but winch them on to the lorry – refuel the truck and pick up everything we need for the job, including road signs to slow cars down when passing. I always wear a protective hat, heavy shoes and special gloves when I'm working. We get back to the depot at 4.30 p.m., which is quite a short working day. And if, for instance, I've had to go to Spurn Point (67 miles from York), it doesn't leave a lot of time to put up poles. Usually though, we can do six to eight poles a day.

I don't really have any direct dealings with the public, but I quite often get asked questions by passers-by about what we're doing, and as it's a pretty interesting procedure, we

Paul enjoys working with heavy machinery.

Once erected, the new pole is made square.

The poles have to be winched on and off the lorry.

sometimes get small gangs of children inter-rupting our work! I sometimes have to knock on doors too, to tell people that we're going to cut them off for a short time while we get the wires down.

The job is certainly better than working in a garage. No two days are the same and we're always working in different places. We have to deal with some unusual problems some-times, such as putting up a pole in a howling gale, and avoiding water pipes when drilling. We spend a fair amount of time putting new poles next to old ones, when the old poles have either been damaged or the lines have to come down for renewal. So we often work with an overhead crew at the same time, which means we have a lot of laughs and really enjoy the work.

Working outdoors can be a bit rough in the winter, especially if I'm working at Spurn Point, on the northern part of the Humber estuary, which is flat and bleak and usually has a strong east wind blowing in from the sea. But I don't mind too much. The poles themselves come mostly from Scandinavia and Scotland. The trees are grown especially to make poles, taking 30 to 70 years to mature for British Telecom's use. The lorry carries up to twelve poles per trip. When an old pole has to come out, the overhead crew take the wires down while my mate and I prepare the new one, with its ladder-rungs and galvanised-steel crosspiece for the top.

The overhead crew can now re-attach the cable to the new pole.

The old pole is withdrawn from the ground by a machine which uses compressed oil and the weight is taken up by the crane on the lorry. The new pole is put into the existing hole, which is then filled with rubble, and hammered down after the pole has been made square. Drilling holes for new poles is done with a large auger.

I also use my HGV licence for another job – driving fire engines in the evenings and at weekends. I have a special bleeper, because as a part-time fireman I'm always on call. If I'm working in or around York I sometimes have to down tools and rush off to fight fires. I would have liked to have been a fireman, but it's really a difficult thing to get into on a full-time basis. I hope within the next two years to become a fitter, but just for now I'm perfectly happy.

Sally Tait
Telephonist

Sally Tait is 22 years old, and did a one-year business studies course before joining British Telecom as a telephonist at York exchange. She finds it is a way of dealing with the public – even if not face to face – and enjoys the friendly working atmosphere at the exchange.

Although I wanted a job which involved meeting the public, working in a telephone exchange is still a way of having contact with people, even though you don't actually get to see them. A reception-telephonist job is interesting and enjoyable, but as an operator with British Telecom my chances of promotion are much better and the pay is also very good.

When I left grammar school I had nine CSEs and didn't really know what to do, so I went to York College of Art and Technology and studied 'O' level English and a one-year business studies course. Part of the course was a reception-telephonist assignment which I really enjoyed. We worked with telex machines and PBX (private branch exchange) switchboards. After college my first job was as a junior switchboard operator for a firm of accountants in York. I thoroughly enjoyed it, but there was no chance of promotion there. I then moved to an estate agents to work a PBX, but was later made redundant, so I went to work part-time in a clothes shop. It was while I was there that I decided to apply to British Telecom. If I wanted to be a telephonist it seemed the obvious choice. I wrote to the general manager's office and the letter was referred to the exchange, as I said I liked using telephones and could type quite well.

My application was processed, with various communications going to and fro by post, such as my application form, medical notes and birth certificate. Then I had an interview with the chief and divisional supervisors which I found quite difficult. I was given a headset, and had to do a voice test, as well as a spelling test of different place names. I then had to read some set phrases, each with a particular emphasis. I was also asked to look up a couple of towns in an alphabetical file of exchanges and codes, and read them

Above *Sally makes out a charging ticket.*

back through the headset. I think my previous experience helped me in the handling of the apparatus, but I've also got a clear speaking voice, am fairly self-confident and was very enthusiastic about the job.

The job turned out to be very different from what I expected. I'd imagined just dealing with directory enquiries or answering 100 lights (calls to the operator) but it covers many other things as well. I've been here two years now, and I'm 22. During the first four weeks, the training supervisor showed us around the building, and told us about British Telecom and how exchanges work. Using a cassette and instruction booklet, we learnt how to receive and answer calls. When we went on to the switchboard for the first time,

the supervisor took all the calls while we listened in, and we watched while she made out all the charging tickets and then filed them. These are tickets noting the details of every chargeable call.

We can start work any time between 7.55 and 10.45 in the morning and leave between 3 p.m. and 6 p.m. when the night staff come on. Being a night-telephonist is a different job altogether. Duties and times are different every week, so we follow a rota.

I arrive at 7.55 a.m. from a small village outside York, where I live with my parents. I bring my own car in and always make sure I'm on time, as being punctual is very important here. I look at the rota to see which switchboard position I'm occupying that day.

Below *Sally uses microfiche at the directory enquiries position.*

Connecting a call through the exchange.

I might be on directory enquiries for two hours, then someone will come and relieve me while I have a fifteen-minute coffee break. After that I look at the rota again and I could be on the switchboard for the rest of the morning. I bring a packed lunch with me, and usually go into town for the rest of the lunch-hour. In the afternoon I may find myself on relief duty, which means taking over in various other positions to give people their tea breaks.

We're kept very busy during the week. There are about forty operators, all girls on the daytime shift, and there's a lovely working atmosphere. Directory enquiries is always a busy duty. The calls here are automatically fed in, so when I sit at the position and plug in, the calls are already lined up for me: I can't choose which one to take.

The '100' position is always busy too. This is the number to dial to talk to an operator if, for instance, you are having trouble dialling; if a number is faulty; if it's engaged and you want the line tested; if you want a 'no reply' test; if you want to use the credit card facility; if it's a Freephone number, and for ADC (advice, duration and charge) calls, when I phone the customer back with the price of a specific call he has made. The big companies tend to be the main users of this last facility.

We do have lots of strange calls, but I'm trained to deal patiently with people and be the same with everyone, whether they are

Above *The directory enquiries position is always busy, with the calls automatically lined up for the operator.*

polite, rude or just peculiar. After I'd been operating for a while, I got to know certain numbers off by heart, such as the local hospitals, social security offices, the university, the major factories, taxi firms, railway stations and so on, because people often just ring us instead of looking the number up in the directory for themselves.

No one here grumbles about the money, but if you're saving up for something special, there's plenty of opportunity to do overtime. On the other hand, if you want someone to fill in for you for a couple of hours because you're going out, or have to go to the dentist,

Sally helps a caller with a problem.

On relief duty, Sally takes over from other operators to give them their breaks.

you can ask someone who's on earlier than you to work the extra hours and actually pay them yourself. Telephone operating is a twenty-four service every day of the year, so we have the opportunity to work bank holidays on double-time and a half, or have a day off in lieu. You can also work over Christmas, which is a smashing time at the exchange: there's a really super atmosphere.

My boss is the chief supervisor in the exchange and if I wanted to move up I'd become an acting supervisor and have to do clerical duties in the exchange, such as updating directories. Alternatively, I could get a transfer to the general manager's office to do clerical duties. Sometimes there are engineering jobs available too. Quite a few of the girls have moved downstairs to ease the engineers' workload, helping them to test for faults.

One part of my job which can be exciting is answering the 999, or emergency calls. There are always two telephonists on this position and the first priority is speed. When someone dials 999, a red light comes up in the exchange, and I answer it promptly and

ask which service (police, fire or ambulance) is required. While I'm putting the caller through, the girl sitting next to me finds out if the number is actually coming from the one the caller has said. We have a way of finding this out.

After I've put the caller through to the police for example, I pass on the number and make sure the police have all the information the caller has given me. People often tend to panic when they dial 999, so I have to be reassuring and make sure they know I'm putting them through as quickly as possible. I've been trained to calm people down when they're distressed. If for some reason the caller doesn't give me the number and I can't pass it on, the police may want to trace it, so I have to contact the special faults engineer and within a few minutes I can have the number where the caller is speaking from. It makes no difference if the caller has put his receiver down, because I can hold the line open by keeping my cord in place until the engineer's voice actually comes on the line asking whether it's the correct one. You always work as quickly as you can, so you hope you're helping to save lives.

There are always lots of social events going on here. Last year I played mixed cricket with the engineers, and the sports and social club is always arranging trips, either abroad, or to events such as the Ideal Home Exhibition. It's so much easier when all the travelling arrangements are made for you, and you go with friends from the exchange.

I like working with a lot of people and I'm very happy here. The only disadvantage of the job is sitting down all day, so I'm into keep-fit and swimming at the moment. I go running every night, because I feel the need to get out to exercise in the fresh air. I usually have a sauna after my keep-fit and I've just taken up photography.

David Smallwood
Trainee technician apprentice

David Smallwood is 18, and has a three-year apprenticeship based at York telephone exchange. His work includes general maintenance of the equipment and correcting faults. David's apprenticeship includes spending time in the different departments within British Telecom, to give him a better picture of how British Telecom works as a whole.

What really made me start thinking seriously about a job with British Telecom, was that I went to an open evening of conducted tours held by British Telecom, and I was so fascinated by the working of a telephone exchange, that I set my heart on joining. I got home and told my dad I wouldn't mind having a go at that sort of thing, and I told the careers teacher too. I spent a lot of time in the careers room at school – the Archbishop Holgate Grammar here in York – and the teacher advised me who to write to for jobs. I wrote about fifteen letters to all the big local engineering firms, because advertisements for apprenticeships hardly ever appeared in the local paper. Halfway through the selection procedure for the electricity board, British Telecom offered me an apprenticeship, so I snapped it up. I later learned that only eight apprentices out of an initial four hundred who applied were taken on by York Telephone Area.

I was 16 then, and had 'O' levels in engineering science, chemistry and English, but I failed maths and physics. I ended up by paying later for not working hard enough at school as I had to do the exams again, studying for two evenings a week at night-school. This was on top of my day-release training which included a night at college, so I was studying three nights a week and having very little social life.

At the interview I was a bag of nerves. The area training officer, who is my boss while I'm an apprentice, asked me about my hobbies. I told him I had built radios from kits, and I also said I'd been round a telephone exchange. I was asked a few technical questions, such as how relays operate, a bit about solenoids, nothing too deep: they just wanted to know if I had a basic understanding of electrical engineering, which I'd studied at school. I also had a test (mainly general knowledge and a few maths problems), and a medical. I'd learned how to sell myself at an interview by chatting to my father and my careers teacher.

It was about two months between the interview and starting work. On my first day I was told to report to an office and once again I was very nervous, but when I arrived I saw a couple of lads I recognised from school, which made me feel a lot more at ease. After a general introduction we all came over to the telephone exchange for lunch, and by then we were already firm friends. In the afternoon we were sent out to look at telephone poles, and at the end of the day I wondered what I'd been worrying about.

Mine is a three year apprenticeship based here at York telephone exchange, and I shall have three years at technical college on day-release, coming out with a TEC in telecommunications. There's an optional further two years studying, which is advisable for future promotions, so I shall certainly do that.

It's a hard apprenticeship, with a lot to learn. The actual exchange lines are put in by a construction group and we, after a certain time, take over the maintenance of the exchange. We have hundreds of diagrams to follow, showing all the wiring, the colour of the wires and their correct positions. The cables also have a colour code, to help sort out where they go, which you're supposed to memorise. It's fairly difficult to learn. You go on three training courses at Otley in your first three years, each one more difficult than the last. The equipment we work with is

Routine maintenance is part of David's daily job.

Other technicians are always on hand to advise.

becoming more technically complicated all the time, but the training officer is very good at explaining things and the other blokes are really helpful as well.

Once you've got a basic understanding of how an exchange works, you're told to go off and do a job on your own and to give them a shout if you have any problems. Sometimes you can be working away, and someone will come by just to see if you're getting on all right. We have instructions produced by British Telecom to work from, which are guidelines for installing and making adjustments to machinery, but if you're stuck the blokes are always willing to stop what they're doing and explain something to you: they're tremendous.

My boss works out a training syllabus for me which sends me around the different divisions within British Telecom so that by the

time I finish my apprenticeship as a technician IIA, I will know how British Telecom fits together and works as one company. I've been out fitting 'phones in houses, helping install telex machines and I've been on the maintenance jointer's job, which involves going into deep holes to repair cables.

I start work at 8 a.m. and finish at 4.30 in the afternoon, with an hour for lunch. The first thing we do each day is to start with a thing called 'routiners'. These are machines which do routine tests on switches in the exchange overnight, while there aren't many calls coming through the exchange. If there is a fault, a docket (a slip of paper giving details) is automatically printed out. In the

Left *David and his training officer refer to the British Telecom instructions over a problem.*

Below *Testing for a fault.*

morning, we sort out all these dockets for the different types of switches in the exchange, go round and find the switch, take it out if necessary and try and correct the fault. The rest of the day is spent in daily maintenance, which includes cleaning and mechanically adjusting all the switches regularly.

The automatic telephone exchange, or 'auto', is split into sections and sub-sections, because it's a main exchange. In the sub-sections are the racks of switches for the whole of York Telephone Area. I have a dust coat to keep dust off all my clothes, and my own dust off the switches. We have to change our footwear when coming into the exchange to help keep the dust level down. Dust is one of the main causes of faults.

At first I was going home with headaches from the constant clatter of the switches, as people dialled and the numbers were automatically routed, but after the first couple of weeks I was used to it. We have an alarm system, so that if a switch goes faulty while in service, a bell rings. I couldn't hear it at first over the noise of the switches. Once I got used to the noise I could pick out this bell quite easily.

It was all a bit confusing at first because British Telecom uses its own technical jargon which is like a foreign language to the beginner. At first I was afraid to ask questions. For instance when I was out putting in subscribers' telephones, I often heard the word 'dis' being used, and I kept wondering what on earth it meant. Obviously I had to find out sometime, so I asked, and it turned out to refer to a disconnection.

I really feel involved with the job now and I wouldn't swop it for anything. The other blokes sometimes ask me what I want to be in the future, and I always say that one day I might be general manager for an entire telephone area, because it is still possible to work

Having gone through his dockets of faults, David attempts to correct them.

your way up from being an apprentice if you work hard and keep your nose clean. I suppose if there's one thing that takes some getting used to, it's going to college, as it's a long day. I'm only just getting a bit more spare time to go to the local youth club, which is attached to the church. I also sing in the church choir and go to Bible study.

The apprenticeship is one with a job at the end of it but I'm on parole all the same, with interviews every so often to make sure that I'm learning things and not just wasting time. I feel confident to tackle almost anything now. Going to college, and learning on the job itself, have certainly made me grow up a lot.

Cathy Hinchey
Clerical officer

Cathy Hinchey is 24 and works in the busy telephone accounts group, one of the biggest departments within York Area. After looking after the accounts of many thousands of telephone subscribers, she has recently changed her duty to take over the accounts of around 1,000 telex customers.

When I left the Bar Convent Grammar School at the age of 17, with five 'O' levels and one CSE, I wanted to become a hotel receptionist. York is always full of sightseers, especially in the summer, and there are lots of hotels to cater for them. Unfortunately, I was told that I was too old, as I would have to be paid an adult wage for what was really a junior job, so I went to York Technical College to do a one-year secretarial course. I failed my typing minimum of 40 words-a-minute, but came out of college with passes in English, audio-typing and office practice.

Very few of the jobs advertised in the local paper were suitable for me, so I started writing letters to firms in the York area. I've always lived in York, and it was knowing all the major companies in the area which helped me when it came to deciding who to write to for a job.

British Telecom originally told me there were no vacancies for clerical officers (for which I had the minimum number of 'O' levels required at the time) but that I would be put on a waiting list. About four weeks later, I had another letter to say that a vacancy for a clerical assistant had arisen.

I didn't exactly shine at the interview, although it was more like a discussion really, to see what sort of person I was, rather than what I knew. I wasn't very good at meeting new people then, so I found it quite difficult. However, I passed the interview and started with British Telecom when I was 18 – I'm 25 now.

The telephone accounts group – we call it TAG for short – may sound pretty dull, but it is actually the second largest department in the building. There's rarely a moment when I'm not busy, and I really enjoy all the bustle. I didn't have to face this big office straight away, as I began in a much smaller

Cathy writes out a subscriber's telephone bill.

Cathy sorts her way through the paper jungle.

one nearby.

For a year I worked in the telephone rentals group, providing rental information to other departments. I came over to the accounts section as a clerical assistant, again for about twelve months. I was then made relief clerical assistant and trained on various jobs within accounts, so that I could fill-in for other people. I didn't want to change my job at the time, but I'm glad I did because it turned out to be a lot more interesting: one week I might be on the manual accounting section, and the next with the legal group, whose job is to chase-up outstanding bills. This occasionally involved going to the law courts to get papers signed.

About three years ago – around the same time as I got married – I was promoted to clerical officer. My husband, Tony, is a higher clerical officer in charge of the data preparation group. There are quite a few couples in the building: it must be down to the nice atmosphere here!

I had three weeks' training in the office, followed by a four week course in Birmingham which gave me a lot of background knowledge. I had a final four weeks of instruction back in the office, after which I was left to get on with the job on my own.

On the accounts duty, I get in at about 8.15 a.m. and look in my diary to see which subscribers' bills require attention; in other words, who has paid and who may need reminding. Each day I go to the visual display unit for my PIF – that's payment information facility. This involves tapping into the VDU the numbers of the subscribers I want to enquire about. The computer then tells me whether they have paid or not. I can make any amendments or add further details to the bills as necessary. After that, I go back to my desk and work through the diary step-by-step. Then I deal with the daily correspondence.

Until recently, I dealt with between 9,000 and 10,000 telephone subscribers, like every clerical officer in my group. With so many accounts, you're busy all day, but of course you don't get 10,000 people querying their bills all at once. The bills are never sent out all together, anyway. They are divided up into categories and dispatched at different times throughout each quarterly period.

Below *With thousands of customers to account for, computers are an absolute necessity.*

A short time ago I moved on to telex accounts. Now I have just over 1,000 accounts to look after, all business customers. The work is still mostly computerized, but each account is more time-consuming than when I was in my previous job. The telephone is constantly ringing in this sort of job, and I receive a lot of letters as well.

The amount of time I spend on the telephone each day depends on how long each

Above *Cathy consults the VDU for up-to-date information on a subscriber's bill.*

enquiry takes to answer. For example, I used to have a few retired people, especially old ladies, who would ring with a basic query, which amounted to nothing really, and then start chatting about the weather and so on. I once had a lady who talked for twenty minutes about her mail-order catalogue just because I happened to mention that I had the same one.

There are always one or two customers

31

If the bills have just gone out, Cathy spends most of her day on the telephone answering queries.

In a big office, there's always someone to help you out.

who, for various reasons, can be very unpleasant. I once had to deal with an old-age pensioner, who actually sounded quite charming on the 'phone, but who was not always honest regarding his financial situation, and his cheques bounced every quarter. He had it worked out to the last hour when we were going to cut his telephone off, so we decided to cut him off immediately we knew the cheques had bounced. He then began to call me up on the same day that the cheques bounced, to say that he would pay in cash – and he always did!

The other duties in my group are private wire duty (looking after customers who have a line continually connected to police stations and the like); balance duty (balancing all the figures from accounts and the cash office each month); radio-paging, public telephone kiosk and temporary line accounts. These temporary lines are often installed for exhibitions and shows, when they are needed for just a week or so. It rarely occurs to me that I'm working for such a vast organization, just that I must keep my own work up to date.

If you keep your eyes and ears open for what jobs are available, you can move around within British Telecom quite a lot. My boss, Ray Garnett, writes annual reports on all the accounts staff in his section, which you can see and query if you want to. The report may or may not suggest that you are suitable for promotion. If you are, you 'take a board', which means having an interview for a higher position. I'm happy with what I'm doing for the time being, but perhaps in a few years I'll try for a board, when I'm older and want more responsibility.

I like the work, and there's a good atmosphere in the office. A welcome break twice a day is the drinks and food trolley which comes round. I was a bit wary of meeting people at first, but you soon get to know everyone. Working here has made a lot of difference to my personality – made me more out-going.

There are always lots of social activities going on, such as mixed football against the general manager's office, discos and car treasure hunts. Then there are my union meetings as well: I belong to the Civil and Public Servants Association.

My husband and I spend most of our spare time decorating and gardening at our house here in York. My father-in-law is a British Telecom engineer, so it's quite a family affair!

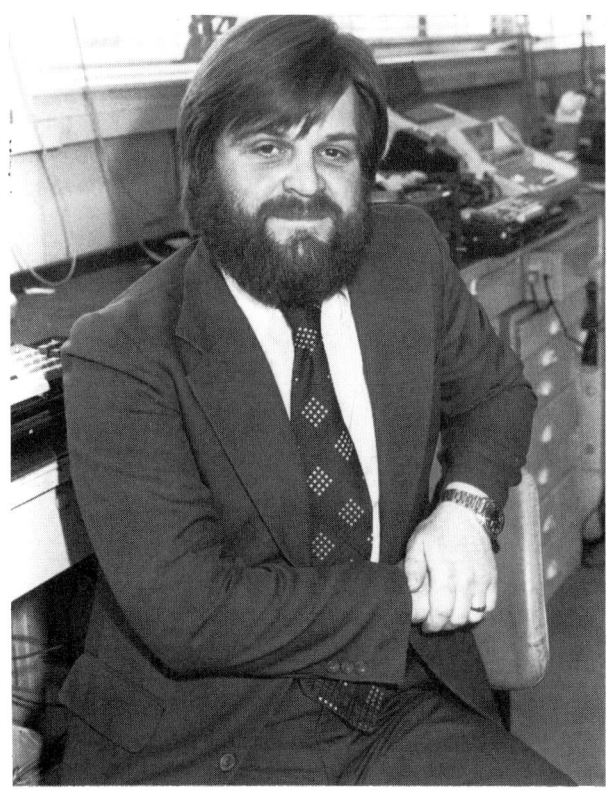

John Dixon
Technical officer, field telex maintenance

John Dixon is 31 and he joined British Telecom straight after he left school. His job is to repair and maintain telex machines, and to make sure the customers are happy with the service their machines give. He is on emergency call-out, twenty-four hours a day.

Telex has turned the world of communications upside down. It's fantastic to think that a written message from York can be received in Hong Kong within a matter of minutes, and I'm glad to be part of such exciting technology. I look after about 150 telex customers and I have to work out my own daily schedule. The job involves a lot of travel about York Telephone Area, which is quite large – about 100 miles from east to west and 70 miles from north to south.

Last year I clocked-up 16,000 miles in my eye-catching, bright yellow van, which I keep at home because I'm always on call. We offer a twenty-four hour service to our telex customers.

I had always been interested in electrical engineering and going after an engineering apprenticeship, partly because my father was a Post Office engineer himself, and partly through the advice of the careers teacher at school. The teacher pointed me towards other areas of engineering so that, as well as writing to the Post Office, I also wrote to British Aerospace and' the Central Electricity Generating Board. I lived in Pocklington, about thirteen miles east of York, and went to the public school there. I left in 1969 when I was 16, with 'O' levels in French, physics, English language, English literature and geography. I was quite strong in physics, which probably helped me get the job, and I later got maths at college.

Both British Aerospace and the Post Office offered me apprenticeships, but the Post Office was my first choice so I went for an interview with the area training officer and the executive engineer in charge of training. I was checked for colour blindness because of all the different coloured cables I have to work with. Colour is very important to us, and anyone who can't tell one colour from another could easily blow himself up.

John arrives at a customer's premises to repair a fault.

As a trainee technician apprentice my first two days were spent on an induction course with one or two others who were starting at the same time as me. We were introduced by the training officer to those people we would be working for; provided with some basic tools; given some idea of basic safety requirements; introduced to the union secretary and made to feel at home. We were also encouraged to ask questions.

My first day was packed full of things to be done. The other apprentices and I sat around a large conference table and we had our photographs taken, with our names under them, which I found a bit disturbing at the time. I also had to sign the Official Secrets Act, as everyone does with British Telecom, since there are certain aspects of the job which cannot be widely known, such as work we do on government property. The first few days were hectic but enjoyable. Nevertheless, when you're only sixteen it's a big change in your life: one day you're a schoolboy, the next

a young man at work. A lot of growing up was done in a very short time.

That was fifteen years ago, but the apprenticeship procedure has changed very little. The first three years of my apprenticeship training were spent on the job and on courses at Otley, some forty miles away, where I had to live in digs. I also went on day-release to college and came out with an intermediate pass City and Guilds, now known as a Technician Education Council certificate.

I was then promoted to technician IIA and put on transmission duties, which is the long distance transmission of communications. For this, we have repeater stations, which contain amplifiers. For example, if you want to talk from York to Leeds, the call would have to be amplified somehow along the way – you can't just put a pair of wires together. After a year at the York repeater station I was made a technical officer in training, which meant passing more training courses and allied courses: in my case, those relating to transmission. So about five and a half years after joining British Telecom, I was promoted to technical officer grade. I'd already done this job on relief duty which meant being temporarily promoted to fill in for others. This means an increase in your salary, so when you are eventually promoted on a permanent basis you can find yourself fairly high up the salary scale.

When I was promoted, I left the repeater station and moved on to telex-maintenance duties, which I've been doing ever since. I'm

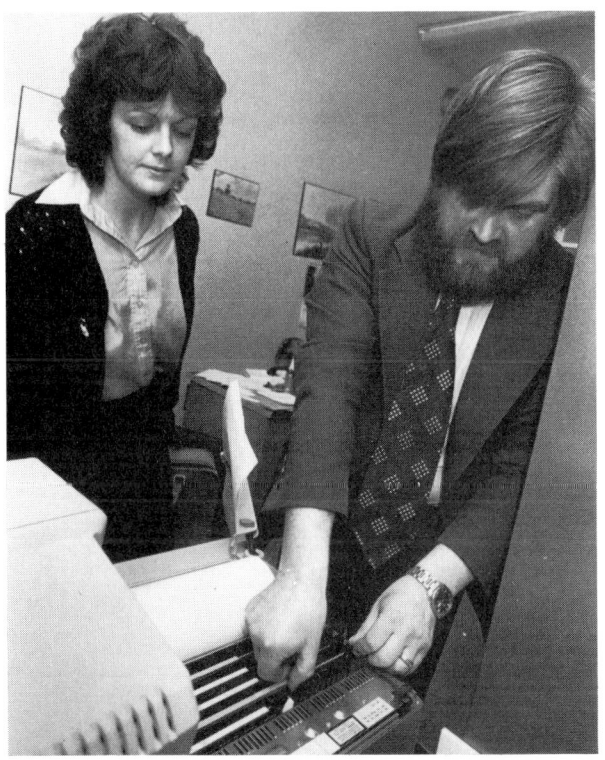

John shows a telex operator the workings of her new machine.

31 now, and the job has changed a lot over the years. I'm on emergency call, available twenty-four hours a day if needed. For instance, if the police want to use their telex in the middle of the night and for some reason it's faulty, they are quite at liberty to ask for attendance immediately. I will get a call from the local repair service control centre to tell me what the customer says is wrong with it. That can happen at any time, but on a normal day, the first thing I do is ring into the telex

Back in the repair workshop, John gets to grips with a fault.

35

exchange to see if any new faults have been reported which are geographically nearer to me than the ones I may have planned to put right on the other side of York. This way I can plan my route properly. After dealing with any faulty machines, I then decide which maintenance visits to make. I also regularly visit customers who have already had telex machines installed, to make sure everyone's happy with them. In the field, we tend to change equipment on a one-to-one basis and the faulty machine is brought back to the main repair workshop in York where we can repair it at leisure. The idea is to get service restored to the customer as quickly as possible.

Telex is a means of transmitting printed information from one place to another, a means by which a person who has a telex machine, can call up anyone else on the world-wide telex network. The chattering machine spewing out paper, like you see on television at the back of the police station, is almost a thing of the past, as the new ones tend to sit there humming quietly. The old telex machines are the electro-mechanical kind, many still giving excellent service. But in the last two years or so the new generation of microprocessor-controlled telexes have appeared on the market. These are the ones which have electronic cards, or circuit boards, and numerous special functions on offer – for instance, one has a visual display unit for message preparation, so that calls can be edited. I did a couple of training courses in London and whenever new models are launched one-day seminars are held at the British Telecom school at Stone, in Staffordshire.

Fault-finding often involves a lot of detective work. I once had to deal with a telex machine which went wrong regularly at 9 o'clock in the morning. It took me three days

Patience and a lot of detective work are sometimes required to trace what needs repairing.

to work out that at 9 o'clock every day, the secretary would come in and brew up the first cup of tea of the day, and every time she switched the kettle on, it gave the poor old telex an electrical shock from the office's

36

faulty main wiring! I also get infuriating problems, such as the machine which would go wrong maybe once a fortnight on just one character, which is important because a telex must be word perfect. This took ages to solve, and turned out to be due to people walking on floorboards above where the wiring ran, so that a protruding nail was pressed into the sheath of the cable just enough to upset the telex when it was working.

With the modern equipment, you learn to keep an open mind, as sometimes the fault can be the operator herself. Once I had to ask tactfully if the telex user would mind very much cutting her nails!

I've been on telex duties now for the past eight years and my interest has been refuelled

John's work helps him to keep abreast of new developments in technology.

with the arrival of the new microprocessing machines. But if I want to go back into the mainstream of telecommunications, the opportunities are there, especially for sideways moves. I'm not yet qualified for promotion to the next grade up. On promotion, I would be involved in more administrative work, and at the moment I prefer getting about and meeting people.

I've recently bought myself a home computer which is quite an aid to me in my job, as it has given me a greater understanding of the equipment we have to work with. I'm fairly happy on the electrical side of it, but with computers there is also the vast software side which I'm not so familiar with. I'm married, with two children. I also like music, model railways, spending time with the kids, and I have a passing interest in maintaining our family car!

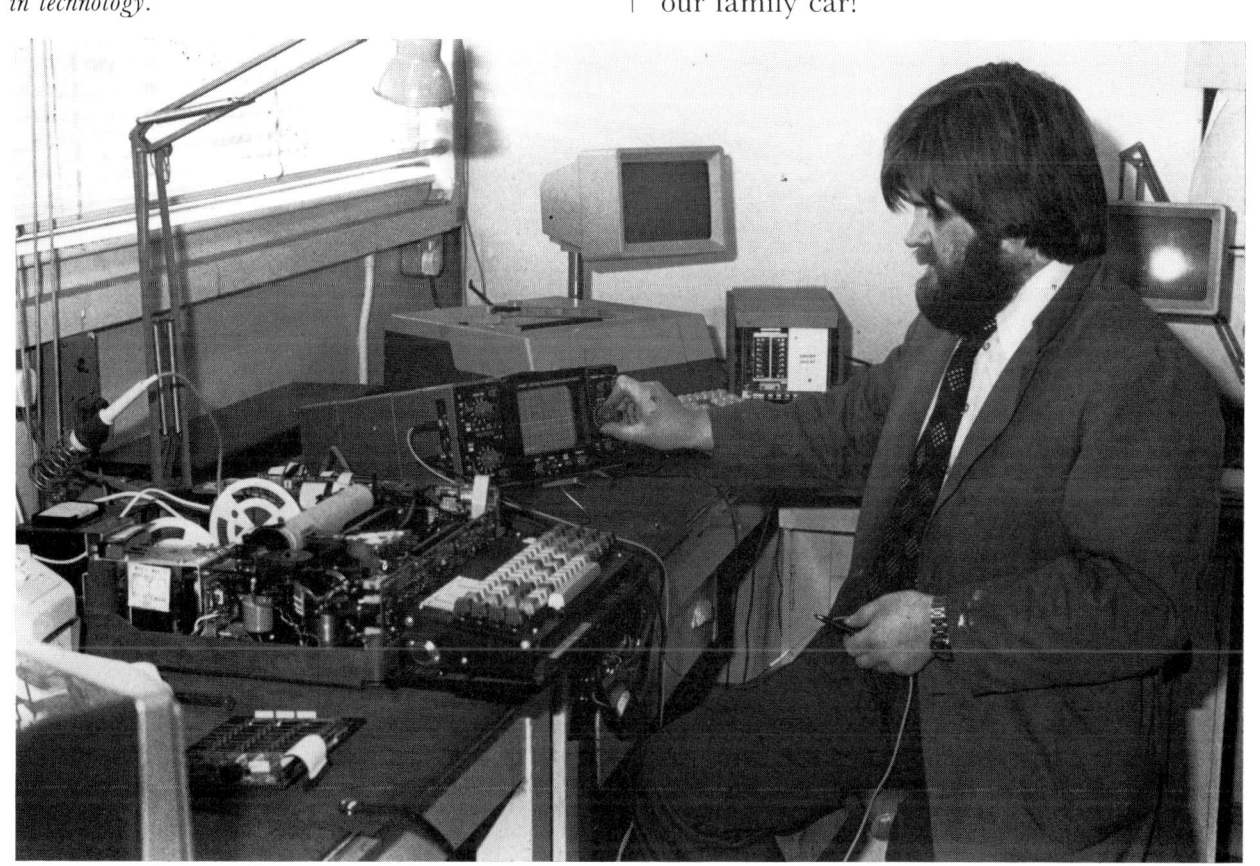

Marion Irving
Senior drawing office assistant

Marion Irving originally worked for British Telecom in London. Now, in the drawing office at York, she makes plans of all telephone cables laid in York Area. There is always plenty of work, as new cable is constantly being laid.

Technical drawing is something I've always been interested in, but I wasn't allowed to take it to exam level at school, so I did it as an extra 'O' level on day-release at college when I'd already started working for British Telecom. That's one of the really good things about this company: the opportunity to study and get on.

I went to a comprehensive school in London, and got two 'O' levels, but before the exam results I went to see the careers teacher who suggested doing something in the field of technical drawing as a job. At school there was only one other girl and myself in a class of forty boys for technical drawing. A British Telecom cartographer came to one of our careers meetings and I got an interview for the job of junior drawing office assistant doing local line records.

I was so petrified (I was just 16 at the time) that I asked my father to come to the interview with me. I had to take some examples of my drawing and printing along. I'd only had basic line drawing and lettering experience at school but I'd drawn parts of tools and machines for the school workshop. The selection procedure lasted two hours, and included a test with various shapes and diagrams, a map-reading exercise, as well as more general questions.

Previously, I'd had no idea that British Telecom even had a drawing office, but I think I got the job largely because of my enthusiasm for technical drawing. When I actually started in 1972, it felt wonderful to be doing what I wanted and getting paid for it as well! I'm 29 now, and still enjoying it.

When I first started work for British Telecom in London, I was put in a training pool for doing simple jobs. I then moved to a group under a leading draughtsman and after about six months was promoted to the position of drawing office assistant. Seven years ago my boyfriend and I moved up to York on a transfer with British Telecom because we couldn't afford to live in London. We married three years later and my husband now works as a technical officer in the planning department, so we can meet for lunch, which is rather nice. There is a small canteen in the building or we can walk over to the main telephone exchange where there is a subsidised staff restaurant for proper meals, which is very good.

There are six instruction books to work through while training in the office, starting from the basics of how to hold your pencil and how to adjust your lamp, and moving on to instructions for doing quite technical drawings. In our office we do local line records, which means recording all the local cables laid, and we have another six books which cover every aspect of the work. The first thing I had to do was learn how to handle maps. We use national grid maps as basic plans for the start of the job, which show you all the streets, and from them we make separate diagrams drawn geographically, making up as many diagrams as are needed for each job.

The training also involved going to college of course, where I took technical drawing 'O' level, and one year of the 'A' level course, and did physics CSE. I also went to metalwork classes at night school so that I could understand some of the machines we were dealing with in technical drawing. I used big lathes, drills, did a bit of welding, made a hack-saw and a metal pencil box.

The job I'm on now is recording cables running between main telephone exchanges.

Marion uses the light box to illuminate her diagram.

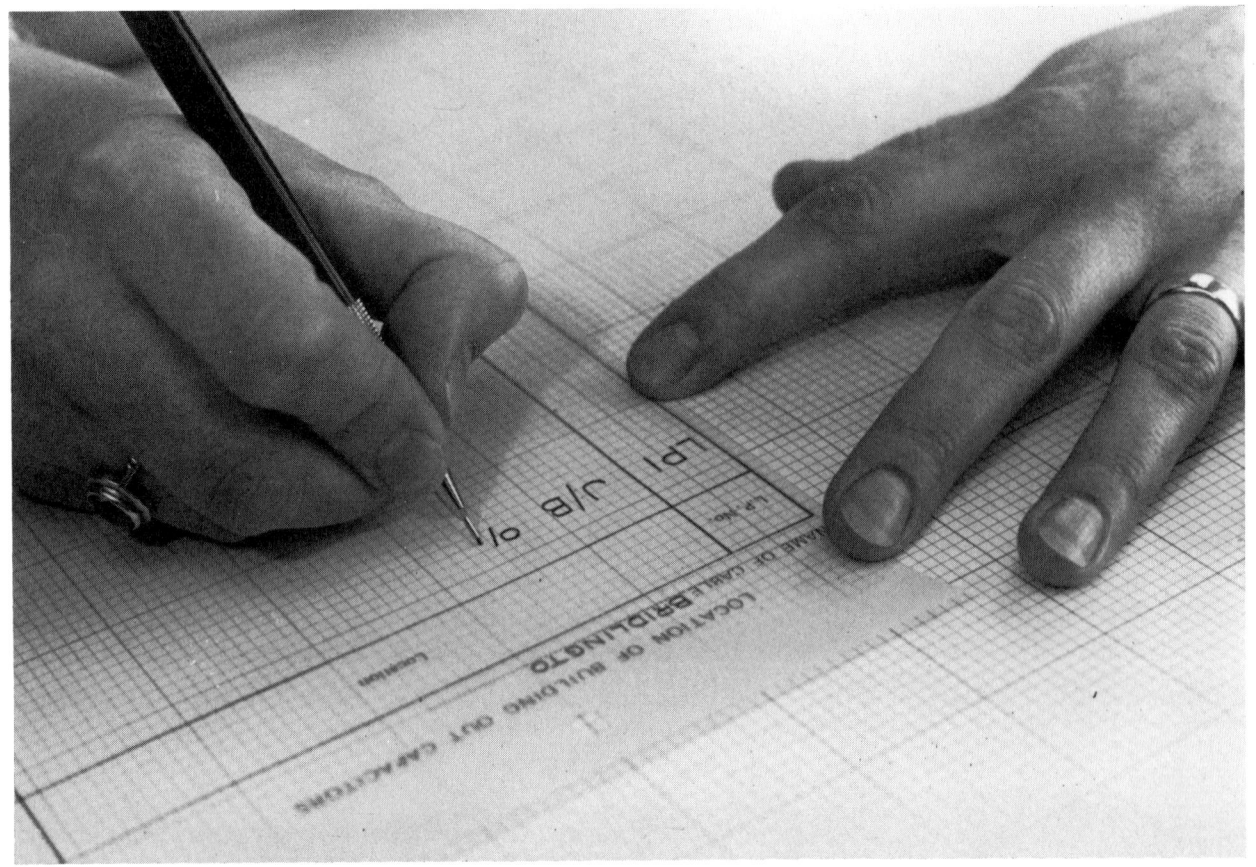

Marion uses graph paper to ensure that she draws her letters to the correct size.

We record for our files all the cables laid from Pickering to the Humber estuary and across the county. We have 121 exchanges in York Area and all cables, right down to those laid to the customer's house, have to be drawn and filed, so that we have an accurate record.

There is always work to do. New cables are constantly being laid to provide more 'phones, and proposals for new cables come to us from the planning department. We make them up a diagram, and when the cables are actually laid, the outside engineers send them back to us to make permanent records for everyone to use.

When I start work at 8.00 a.m., the first thing I do is to take the cover off my drawing board and lay everything out. Every line has to be perfectly drawn and absolutely accurate, and all my letters up to a set standard.

When I have finished a diagram it goes to the print-room for prints to be made and distributed to all those whose work is affected by my new layout sheets. Eighteen of us work on the drawing boards and we have two draughtsmen. We've just had two lads join us but the rest are girls. I think girls have a lot of patience and perseverance for this type of work. I've noticed that it's taken the lads a lot longer to get the hang of it, but the atmosphere is more fun with the lads in here!

All the diagrams are kept in fireproof cabinets and each one is taken out as and when needed, and filed in the correct order again when finished with: otherwise you could spend all day looking for it. I'm con-

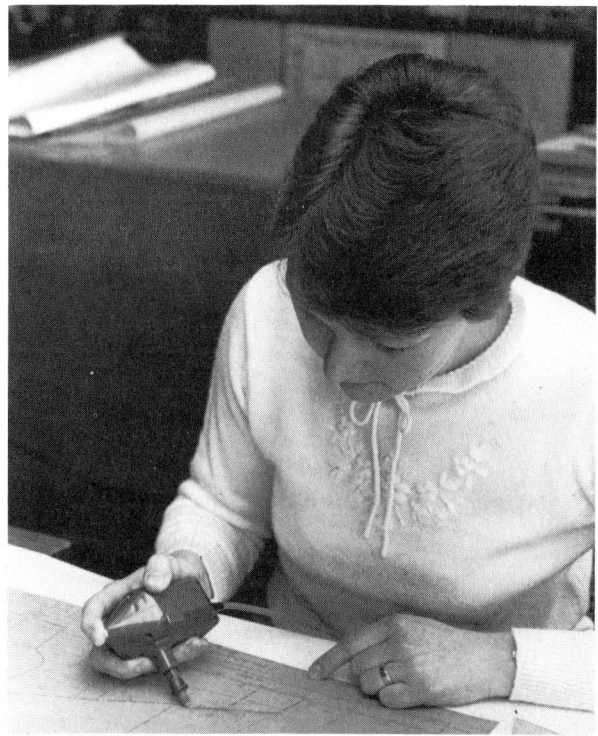

If you make a mistake, it's not the end of the world!

stantly getting up and down, fetching drawings from the files, and returning them. Each person in the group provides or records different information on the maps. Local councils and water authorities doing work in the area also send us plans for us to mark where our cables are, so that a digger won't slice through one and cause damage.

Like most people I do have some days when nothing seems to go right, but fortunately they don't occur that often. It's good to know my work is so important to the Area. If my drawings were incorrect it would cause problems for a lot of people. Everything which belongs to British Telecom either in the ground, or overhead, is shown on our plans.

When we used linen to draw on, I had several accidents spilling my tea or coffee, or a bottle of ink, which ruined the wax surface of the cloth. Now we use a polyester film,

which is super to work on. You can see through it and rub out your pencil marks as often as you like.

My job is challenging and you have to put your mind to it. I could go on to become a draughtsman as I've been senior drawing office assistant for the past three years now, but I would need more technical qualifications, and draughtsmen are usually recruited from outside anyway. It's good to have a job and know British Telecom is there to look after you, but it is a little frightening to think of the possibility of being made redundant, as it wouldn't be easy to find similar work outside.

At the moment I've got plenty to do, especially since I'm on my union committee. My husband and I cycle in every day from our home in Dunnington, five miles from York. We sold our car four years ago and now cycle everywhere. The countryside around here is beautiful for cycling because it is so flat. We've both got racing bikes now but we used to have a tandem, which

Marion works out a map to scale.

we once cycled to London on from here. On another occasion we set off to cycle to London for my sister's wedding. It took us three days to get to Northampton, and we were so exhausted when we got there that we cheated and caught the train. We spend all our holidays cycling and we go outdoor bowling in the summer and run an indoor carpet bowling section in the winter.

Left *Maps are filed in the fire-proof cabinets according to geographical area, for easy reference.*

Below *Marion consults a colleague over a county council map.*

John Baker
Marketing accounts executive

John Baker is 26 years old, and sells British Telecom's products and services within his own 40 square mile patch. He is York Area's top salesman. Because other firms are now allowed to compete in the telecommunications market, competition is getting tougher, but John finds he thrives on the pressure.

Although there is always a lot of pressure on you if you work in the sales department, especially now that British Telecom is having to compete with other telecommunications businesses, I seem to thrive on it. I have to keep on top of my work, and make sure that not only are all the customers in my forty-square-mile patch happy, but that each day's appointments and paperwork are cleared before the next morning.

As far as selling business equipment goes, I deal with all the larger systems of more than four lines. I'm York's top salesman, which does make me feel a little bit proud of myself, considering this job was initially a shot in the dark for me.

I went to a grammar school in Chesterfield, Derbyshire, and left when I was nearly 17, with only two 'O' levels. I got a job soon after leaving, as postal assistant at the General Post Office. Then on day-release I managed to get a couple more 'O' levels, in maths and physics. About eighteen months after joining, I was made postal officer and transferred to the Accountant General Department (AGD) at Chesterfield. This is where every postmaster in the country has to send his accounts at the end of each week. We were, more or less, auditors for the accounts and sent out error notices if accounts didn't balance. After two years I was pretty fed up with this job. Fortunately vacancies for sales reps with British Telecom in York were advertised in the local Post Office Gazette.

The interview was very run-of-the-mill and I can't remember coming away feeling particularly pleased with myself. A panel of three asked me a lot of questions I couldn't answer because they related me to a postman's situation. Everyone thinks of staff in the Post Office as either sitting behind a counter or dealing with mail, neither of which I knew anything about. The questioning was clever, starting off with how to wire plugs and leading on to why you do it that way, gradually making the questions more and more specific, putting the pressure on.

My reactions must have been the right ones, as they gave me the job. That was four years ago now, and I was one of the only six chosen out of the original 156 who applied for the job. I can honestly say I haven't been bored since day one. In sales you've got to be able to communicate with everybody, from a managing director to someone – like a person I've just done business with – who uses bad language as part of his normal conversation. I like meeting people and manage to get along with almost everyone.

John and his sales manager get together for a chat about business in the York area.

However, it was about six months after starting with British Telecom before I went out and met people on my own. There was a lot of training to go through, because I knew absolutely nothing about telephones when I joined. I came to York on the train from Chesterfield and booked into some lodgings. My wife, who was having our first child, came on later. I had two weeks training in York, then three weeks in London, which was the first time I'd been in a big city for any length of time. Then it was back to York for another two weeks, and down to London for a final three. In York, the training involved going out to telephone exchanges, meeting engineers, going out with reps, looking into the paperwork side, and trying to find out about the customers I would be dealing with, and what they actually did. In London we

John on his way to visit a factory.

learned about all the different types of equipment which we would cover in our work. Even then you only scratch the surface of what there is to learn about telecommunications. About two years ago the whole of the field sales group was re-evaluated and the sales rep grade almost disappeared. We all re-applied for the new jobs as marketing sales reps and marketing accounts executives (MAEs). I was promoted last June to MAE, and I'm now 26 years old.

I work from home and only come into the office once or twice a week. I generate my own sales and I have many existing customers. But if a new factory opened in York for example, they would get in touch with our sales office for telephones. The sales office would then inform me, and I would establish contact with the customer and go and see him to discuss his requirements. Meanwhile, he could also be discussing his need for a switchboard or telex with a firm outside British Telecom, so the selling situation now means being able to persuade him that British Telecom's system is better than anyone else's. I have a target selling figure which I have to achieve, and I can earn a commission on my sales, but it's getting harder as we are now in a competitive market, and a more aggressive one. I don't mind it though: in fact I enjoy the challenge which the job offers.

In the mornings I ring into the office to see if there are any messages for me. From these messages I might find that there are engineers, customers or other sales staff wanting to speak to me, so I will ring round and solve as many queries as possible. A percentage of my 'phone bill and rental fee is paid by British Telecom. I also have post delivered to my home instead of to the office. I carry a radio-pager on me, through which I can be contacted if anything urgent comes up. When it 'bleeps' I have to get to the nearest 'phone

Totting up the costs for a customer.

Above *John has to write a report on each visit he makes, which often means taking work home with him.*

and ring the office to find out what the problem is. I haven't any staff under me and I'm fairly independent in my work, as I answer only to the field sales manager.

After contacting the office, I check my diary to see what my first appointment for the day is. For example, if it is with Rainbow Ltd, I get into my company car and go off to see my contact there, with whom I will soon be on first name terms. The customer may be looking to add more telephone lines to his present system, with the possibility of bringing the rest of his equipment up to date. The firm in question produces travel brochures and deals with holiday bookings, so they may want to make themselves more efficient

through telephone-answering time and may wish to discuss a system which would give them this. The visit could last anything from 45 minutes to a whole day. At the end of the day, I have to write a report on each visit I have made.

When big structural alterations are needed for a system to be installed, I might have to get in the external planners if more cable is required, or external surveyors if lines have to run between buildings. I'm the middle-

Below *Looking at a system in York's business centre.*

John goes through his messages in the sales office.

John examines the sales figures.

man in all of this. I send notes, or speak to the British Telecom people concerned, and sometimes I get them all together to discuss the job in hand. My job is very varied and each day is different. The pace can often get quite hectic, and in one of these busy moments I once drove over my own briefcase. It's the pressure, you know!

Some days I can finish at 3 or 4 o'clock in the afternoon. But every night there is written work to do and sometimes I'm still doing my paperwork after midnight. I get five weeks' holiday a year, which I find I need, and we normally take our holidays in this country as it means that we can use the company car.

We have two children now, so with them and the job I have little time for sport, which I used to be quite good at, especially football. I'm really out of training now, although I still play football occasionally in Pocklington, which is where we live, about 15 miles out of York.

Beverley Tebbutt Commercial officer

Beverley Tebbutt deals with requests for new telephones to be installed. She originally wanted to be a PE teacher, but as she now has a job which she enjoys and which still enables her to pursue her sporting interests, she has no regrets.

One of the great loves of my life is sport, and I left school wanting to be a PE teacher. Although that idea didn't work out, I couldn't have ended up in a better company for my sport, because British Telecom actively encourages its staff to get involved in sporting activities. I now have the best of two worlds: a job which I thoroughly enjoy and the opportunity to represent British Telecom's North East Region in netball and badminton.

I left Fulford Comprehensive School in York at the age of 18, with nine 'O' levels and an 'A' level in English. I went to work temporarily for a local engineering company where my sister worked, while I waited to get into Sheffield College for PE training. I was in the payroll department, calculating holiday pay and taxes with the help of a computer. In the end I was asked to stay on and I eventually gave up the idea of going to college.

The job wasn't very demanding, so after two years I applied for a job as clerical officer with British Telecom, which I saw advertised in the York evening paper. I was lucky, as I think I was one of the last people to come in as a clerical officer: most start as clerical assistants now. I wanted the job because I was getting married and we needed money to help with the mortgage on a house, and also because it offered better prospects of promotion in the future.

The interview, which was really a question and answer session, was taken by the personnel manager and the clerical training officer. I think my friendly manner and the fact that I had a voice well suited to telephone work helped me get the job. I was 21 at the time and I've now been with British Telecom for eight years.

My first two days were spent gaining a simple idea of what British Telecom is all

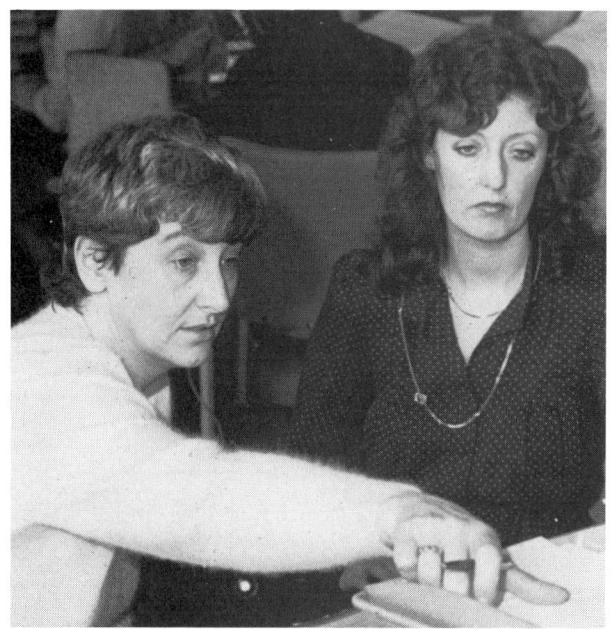

Beverley goes through some work with her supervisor.

The 'phone rarely stops ringing during the day.

about and the basics of the telephone service. I thought I would automatically be put in the wages department but I went to sales instead. The clerical officer post you apply for is a general one, and once you have been accepted, you are placed wherever there happens to be a vacancy.

I had seventeen weeks' training altogether, the last two being at a training school in Manchester, and then I was put on my duty. After about two years I was asked to become a clerical training officer, so I spent several years training others. When my grade of job was divided into commercial and clerical officers I opted for the commercial side. I still didn't have my own particular duty though, as I would go and sit with the trainees while they were learning. Last October I felt I'd had enough of the training side, and wanted to be given a duty and desk of my own again, so I asked if I could have a change from training.

I feel much more settled now. We are on a 'flexi-time' system, which means I can start

any time between 7.30 and 9.30 in the morning. I aim for 8.15, as I have to drive from Wilberfoss, a village nine miles out of York.

Making out an advice note has to be neat, fast and accurate.

The first thing I do when I get in is to look through the post and pick out anything that needs urgent attention. People are always ringing up asking to have new telephones installed. My own telephone rarely stops ringing and I often spend virtually all day on it. I take down the orders, process them, and

then issue an advice note: a master copy which is then duplicated nine times and goes out to the directories, engineers, accounts, the people in the exchange and all the other departments involved.

I cover the Harrogate area, and I deal with all one and two line customers. I'm in the office most of the time, going out very occasionally to exhibitions. The advice note I issue when a customer wants a telephone contains their name and address; another address if the bills are to go to a different one; a telephone number (I keep a list of numbers for new lines); the charge to be recorded on the computer; and how the customer wants to be listed in the directory. All the information on my master copy has to be one hundred per cent correct, so it's fortunate that I've got neat, clear handwriting. I'm the first person in British Telecom that the customers encounter, and usually the only person they get to know, apart from the engineer actually installing the 'phones, so I have to be as pleasant as possible over the telephone. I have to

Between telephone calls, Beverley catches up on processing the sales.

confirm everything in writing to the customer, and later follow it up to find out whether the customer is satisfied or has any complaints. As I work with just one area, I'm known to

All the customers' records are on hand.

Beverley sorts out some filing for the clerical assistant.

my customers by my Christian name, which I think gives a nice personal touch to the job.

On the business side, we have ten commercial and two relief officers. We also have a clerical assistant who does all the photocopying and filing. My boss, who is really a team manager, is a telecom superintendent, and this would be my next step of promotion, unless I decide I'd like to actually go out on the road and try my hand at selling. I've been out with the sales reps a few times and I did enjoy meeting people. Before we had the business centre in York, I helped staff a business sales bureau here, which I loved doing. Learning about all the different telephone systems is really just a matter of reading all the leaflets which come round, but an even better way is to try them out for yourself in the business centre.

I am always very busy in my work and the day usually flies by. I couldn't stand a clock-watching job. There's always something amusing going on. People write poems to us occasionally, just like on Esther Rantzen's *That's Life* programme. I had one lady customer, who wrote me a brilliant poem about Buzby, which I kept. She was obviously having trouble with her telephone, but she saw the funny side and put pen to paper.

My husband works for the Department of the Environment in Hull. We both have our own cars now because it was so inconvenient for me to travel in by bus all the time. I've never looked back since I started working for British Telecom although I'm not as ambitious as I used to be. I'm now 29, and I really think I'd like to have a family. This is a job I could come back to afterwards.

The difficulty at the moment is finding time to follow all my sporting interests. I play netball in the York League, ladies cricket, mixed hockey, tennis, and badminton three times a week: in fact, my weekends revolve around sport. I was presented with a brooch by British Telecom for representing the North East Region on a national level more than five times. I am allowed to go to matches on paid leave, and unless I'm very, very busy in sales, I can usually get afternoons off to go to tournaments.

Ian Allison
Contracts manager

Ian Allison joined British Telecom as a 'direct entrant' after leaving Durham University with an honours degree in geography. He has to draw up contracts with outside firms whenever there is digging or building work to be done. He considers that he has a good job at the age of 25.

'm a Cumbrian, born and bred. Although I seem to have followed a pretty straightforward and usual path into the job of contracts manager for British Telecom here in York, it was nothing like as planned as it sounds. I think I was just in the right place at the right time. I was lucky to get a job like this, which suits my own personality down to the ground, and is quite a responsible position to hold at the age of 25. Even so, I've had to accept the restrictions of working for such a big organization.

I'm what British Telecom calls a 'direct entrant', which means that I have come straight in as a first-level manager, with a degree or similar qualification (in my case, an honours degree in geography from Durham University).

I left school with four 'A' level passes, and during my last year I applied to universities, as did most of my friends, although I wasn't absolutely sure I wanted to go. In the time between applying and hearing about a place, I changed my mind, took a year off and re-applied to university later. During that year I worked at a local shoe factory doing odd jobs and driving vans. It was an enjoyable break from studying, but I felt I had to do something constructive, so I left home when I was 19 for the three-year course at Durham.

At about Christmas-time of my final year at university, most people were starting to worry about getting jobs after they'd finished, so I decided to write to British Telecom, among others. The university had a careers service, with all types of information available, and one or two jobs caught my eye. The main thing was to get a job at that stage – any job. There's always that feeling that your friends have been working since they left school and you're getting left behind, however well-qualified you might be.

I really wanted to work in a national park

Ian spends a lot of time on the telephone to contractors and other British Telecom staff.

– something loosely related to geography or recreational management – but I quickly realised that it wasn't on unless I had another qualification, which I wasn't prepared to study for at the time. Once I'd accepted that fact, I got down to considering the more realistic alternatives.

As well as filling in an application form for a first-level management post with British Telecom, I also tried the British Shoe Corporation, the Waterways Board and the Yorkshire Electricity Board, but I pulled out of these before the selection procedure had got very far. I was invited to Leeds for an interview with British Telecom, but this was really just a written test, similar to a standard Civil Service aptitude test, I suppose. I got through

that and then had to attend a day of formal interviews. I still had no idea of the specific job I wanted to do. By the time of the next interview, again at Leeds, I had made a preference for working in North East. I was offered an administrative post, although they weren't sure where it would be. It seemed on the cards that the job would be in London, but as luck would have it, the contracts manager post in York came up. All this took about three months, and that was nearly four years ago now.

I found somewhere to live about four miles out of York, which I shared with the owner, and I used to come in to work on my push bike. After a few months I found lodgings in York, and then last summer I bought a house. I'm still single.

My first day was quite awful really. I didn't

know York very well, and I didn't know anybody who lived there, either. I just turned up at this office and spent the day saying hello to people. I felt like a fish out of water!

The contracts manager's job is basically a financial one. I arrange and look after all the contracts within York Telephone Area. A contract is a legally binding document which must be honoured by all the parties involved, and may be set up for a whole variety of reasons, from installing new cables underground to putting a new roof on an exchange.

If, for instance, there's a new housing estate which will need telephones installed, cable has to be laid underground. I arrange for the digging to be done by an outside contractor, as British Telecom itself doesn't employ large numbers of labourers. I negotiate and place the contract, and I'm the link between the planners and the work actually getting done.

A map in the office is a necessity.

A visual display unit makes contract reference easier.

55

When I started, I only had about a week's desk training, and it was some time before I was confident about what I was doing, as there is so much technical information to learn. I also have to meet the public a lot in my job, and so the first three months were pretty difficult for me. It was then that disasters could have occurred, like someone digging up the wrong piece of road and an irate householder falling down the hole. Thankfully, nothing like that happened – possibly due more to luck than judgement! The legal side of the contract is very important: I've had no legal training but the job is well documented, as the procedure in this area is much the same as in any other telephone area.

All the details of the contracts are stored in circular files.

When I get in, at about 8.30 a.m., I sort out anything new which may have come up, and arrange to see people, or telephone them before they go out. I check to see if there is anything diaried for the day, such as a meeting. I may have a new contractor to see who has never worked for British Telecom before, so I'll arrange to meet him and put out feelers to find out if he's the sort of chap we might want. I'll perhaps review the work programme with the planners, to see if we can cope. As a first-level manager, I'm responsible for three clerical officers and a clerical assistant. I have to sign all their work, which takes up a fair bit of my time.

There's a lot of paperwork attached to my job but I also go out quite often. The workload is growing and changing all the time. I'm

Ian goes out to check work in progress in one of York's busy main streets.

responsible for all the telephone kiosks in the area (we have 1,100 of them), including the painting, cleaning and collection of money from them. Not personally, of course, but I must arrange for the work to be done. I'm also involved with the maintenance of buildings, offices, exchanges: in fact anything that needs a contract.

British Telecom as a whole is highly structured, and you have to be at a certain level for a given amount of time before you are considered eligible for promotion. Even if I was absolutely wonderful at my job long before I'd been in it for the stated time period, I'd still have to wait for promotion. I've just about served long enough in my present position, and the most likely thing to happen is that I'll apply for a job within British Telecom which I see advertised internally.

As far as York goes, I'd like to stay here because it's such a lovely place, but I've come to accept that I'll almost certainly have to move for promotion. I'll miss playing football for the local team and for York Telephone Area, as well as running along the riverbank.

I enjoy my job most of the time. Despite the restrictions, I concede that British Telecom is changing quickly now – and for the better. As for the future, I think I'll have to do some more studying, because British Telecom is becoming very specialised. When I started with British Telecom, they simply wanted young people with potential. Now they appear to want young people to have a specific qualification, whether it be in computers, accountancy or whatever.

Ian asks if the work is likely to be finished on time.

Dave Bennett
Exchange manager

Dave Bennett has been with British Telecom for 25 years, and has worked his way up through the grades to exchange manager. He is responsible for 32 exchanges and he aims to get the failure rate for calls going through his exchanges as low as possible.

These days, I would strongly advise any young lad or girl who is leaving school at 16 with nine 'O' levels, as I did, to stay on and take 'A' levels and possibly go on to university as well. By getting more qualifications they could enter British Telecom at the grade I'm in now. It took me fifteen years to reach this grade, from starting as a 'youth-in-training' (as an apprentice was then called) in 1958 to my promotion in 1973. I'm 41 now, and as I've been in this grade for ten years, I'm just eligible to be considered for promotion to executive engineer.

Having said that, I've enjoyed my career with British Telecom immensely, and have few regrets. It is still possible, in spite of the rapidly changing nature of British Telecom, to come in as an apprentice and work your way up through the ranks. My own 'youth-in-training' job with the Post Office (which British Telecom used to be part of) was advertised in the paper, and I followed it up because I thought it sounded as if it offered a promising future. I was given a written test and then short-listed for an interview. At the interview, I was asked about the workings of an internal combustion engine and how a telephone functions, both of which I knew a little about from school. I was offered a job in Sheffield and gladly accepted.

My first day was bewildering to say the least. Sheffield was a city I didn't know at all, and finding the engineering centre was a test in itself! I arrived there, only to find that no one really expected me. I'd already been into the area office to sign a number of forms, and be kitted-out with a few tools, and measured for protective clothing in the stores. The first day was a bit of a let-down but things soon picked up.

The apprenticeship was a two-year one, during which time I spent one day a week at Sheffield Technical College, with evening

The computer monitors how the exchanges are performing.

classes on the same day as well. At the end of the apprenticeship, I was up-graded to technician IIA, although I continued to study for a further two years. I reported to the fitting group for a three-month spell fitting switchboards in customers' premises, mainly in large businesses, such as the Sheffield Steel Works. I spent the following six months as a linesman, clearing faults on lines laid to houses.

About nine months into the training programme, I was asked if I'd like to be transferred to the Barnsley exchange. I was 16 at the time and still living with my parents, so the idea appealed to me very much. So the next two years were at Barnsley doing basic routine maintenance on electro-mechanical switching equipment; changing small instrument parts; cleaning contacts on electrical switches and that sort of thing. The Strowger equipment in the exchanges is very noisy, not loud enough to damage your ears mind you, but the noise is there continuously – like hundreds of typewriters going at the same time.

The next step up was to the grade of technical officer, and again I was promoted from within the Barnsley exchange, which was quite sizeable then, serving between 7,000 and 8,000 subscribers. British Telecom is just installing one of the latest electronic systems there now, which can deal with between 20,000 and 30,000 lines. My duties changed with this promotion, as I was working on my own, doing more complex work, and going out to maintain small private automatic exchanges.

Now I'm responsible for thirty-two exchanges in an area of around 1,000 square miles. I have an office at the Goole exchange and am responsible for nineteen staff, including one apprentice (they are moved around the area for their training) and a mixture of technical officers and technicians.

One of my main tasks is monitoring how the exchanges are performing and making sure that the public is able to make the phone calls it wants to. We have computer-controlled equipment which generates artificial calls into every exchange, and between exchanges, so that it can produce a complete test pattern of all the traffic we are likely to carry. It

Right *Dave has his own office at the Goole exchange.*

Below *Discussing the cause of a fault with one of his staff.*

monitors what happens to the calls and will tell us, for example, that a percentage of all calls going through a particular exchange have failed. We set ourselves targets each year to try and improve on that performance. We are currently aiming for a 0.3 per cent failure rate, which means only three calls failing in every thousand. A lot of our exchanges

Maintaining the high performance levels of his exchanges is Dave's main function.

achieve that target but just one item of equipment failing can change that picture to 50 or 60 calls failing in a thousand, which is nothing short of disastrous for us.

Another aspect of my job is supervising the people under me. My staff are scattered widely so I tend to talk to the people at Goole very early in the morning and then spend most of the rest of the day in contact with staff in other parts of my area. We have radio-pagers for some of the staff, so they can be

contacted quickly. Once I've spoken to the lads at Goole my next task is to review the performances of the previous day and contact various members of staff. We do have the occasional drama, like the near-disaster a couple of years back when Selby town centre, where we have an exchange, was threatened by floods when the river broke its banks. If the exchange had flooded, it would have cut the town off completely.

We took urgent steps to sandbag the exchange all through the night, drafted pumps in and made a lot of detailed plans to cover any eventuality. The local council even called in the army and were actually ready to evacuate the town if necessary. Then we watched and waited, while the water level rose. Fortunately it began to subside before it could do much harm.

That was a fairly unique event but a more common crisis would be an exchange being isolated for one reason or another, and this occurs often enough for it to be part of the day-to-day job. This can be caused by a power failure on our own power equipment, which would switch the exchange off, or a main cable fault underground. These cables are the lifelines of the telephone network. The driver of a mechanical digger, who's not paying attention when he's digging, can cause a tremendous amount of damage. This actually happens far more often than you'd imagine.

I feel I'm particularly suited to this job because I enjoy the technical side of it, and I'm the sort of person who likes to get hold of a problem and stick with it until it's solved. You need to have an enquiring and ferreting mind for this job.

Even so, at 5.15 p.m. each day, I'm glad to switch off (if you'll pardon the pun), go home and relax. I live near Goole, with my wife and four children, and as I'm on call all the time, I sometimes have to turn out at night. In my spare time I'm a youth club leader and am very keen on rock climbing and mountaineering. I'm working hard to qualify myself to teach rock climbing to youth club members. I'm also a member of my local parish council, where I try and avoid conversations on crossed lines!

Dave spends one day a week out of the office, visiting other exchanges.

Norman Williams
Area network service manager

Norman Williams has reached his present position from starting as a youth-in-training in 1949. He oversees 240 staff and is responsible for the maintenance of York Area's external telephone network.

What I enjoy most about my job is having to deal quickly with a potential catastrophe. This means dropping everything else I may be doing at the time. It's rare for any two days to be the same. I never know what might happen, and it's the very immediacy and unpredictability of the situations which arise that I find challenging and exciting. For instance, in March of last year, my staff had no sooner repaired the damage caused by 90 m.p.h. gales, than we had snow blizzards to contend with. This is a mainly rural area and engineers worked like Trojans to reach cut-off farms to repair faults. The satisfaction of finding that my staff and I have coped with a crisis, or averted one, is easily the most rewarding aspect of my job.

As area network service manager, my responsibility is to maintain York Area's external telephone network, from the customers' premises to the local telephone exchange. This includes the repair-service control centres (where telephone faults are reported by the customer and processed until cleared to the customer's satisfaction); the workforce responsible for the maintenance of external equipment and the apparatus in customers' premises; and the area's public kiosks.

I control 240 staff in the network service division, with the help of 11 first-level managers. My boss is the area network manager, and is on the area board. It has taken me 34 years to reach this position, as I joined as a 'youth-in-training' at Middlesbrough in 1949, when I was 16. When I left grammar school in Stockton-on-Tees, I had no idea what job I wanted to do, except that it had to be engineering-orientated. I had a good start because I had eight 'O' levels, and I joined a road haulage firm as a junior clerk: I was 15 at the time.

Later on, I began applying for other jobs,

but after reading the literature about Post Office engineering from the employment office, I became interested in what it had to offer.

I remember thoroughly enjoying the interview, but my first few days were bemusing to say the least. The size of the organization surprised me and it took a while to see exactly where I fitted in. However, the training helped sort me out, as I spent set periods of time in all the different engineering departments in this telephone area. At the end of each period of training, a report was written about me and presented to the training officer to make sure that I'd grasped the right idea.

I also went away on a couple of courses: study was positively encouraged. I attended

Below *Norman's job is overseeing all external equipment, including underground cable.*

Above *Norman checks on a faulty line with an operator.*

day-release and evening classes for some years. In fact, I studied from 1953 to 1963, by which time I'd gained a full Technological Certificate in telecommunications. Since then I've also taken a Bachelor of Arts course in technology with the Open University, for which British Telecom paid a percentage of the fees.

In the early 1950s I joined the Royal Signals, to do my National Service, and when I returned to British Telecom I was promoted to technician. I was later promoted to technical officer, and in 1963 to a first-level management post, as assistant executive engineer at Telecommunications Headquarters in London. After seven years I transferred back to the North East Region's headquarters at Leeds, and was made executive engineer six

Back in his office, Norman spends a lot of time on the telephone.

years later. In 1980 I transferred to York Area, and my present job. I'm 50 now.

It's very difficult for me to describe a typical day's work because events are always occurring that cannot be foreseen. For example, if a large cable has been damaged by road works, then hundreds of telephones could be out of order. These must be restored as quickly as possible, so I have to give priority to ensuring that all resources are organized efficiently to deal with such a case.

Similarly, storms can cause a lot of damage to the external equipment, and a lot of time is spent trying to keep customers' telephone lines in service. If there are no major problems to be dealt with, I start the day by looking through the mail and checking the up-to-date situation on faults. Daily reports on the number of faults on telephone lines are submitted to me, and I have to make sure that our resources are sufficient to clear them properly.

Another of my tasks is to keep a check on the financial performance of my department. By referring to man-hours and money spent over the last month, including overtime, I can see whether my first-level managers are keeping within the financial limits we have been set.

With 240 staff, my job covers some aspects of personnel management, such as discipline, transfers, safety at work and the staff appraisal reports. I also have to work out an overall strategy, if I am to carry out the policies as laid down by the general manager and the

With 240 staff under him, Norman spends a lot of time making out their reports.

area board. This involves me in meetings with my own managers as well as managers from other divisions. I sit on various committees, some of which involve trade unions. I also belong to the Society of Telecommunications Executives, and I do a limited amount of negotiating with trade union branch secretaries.

I am mostly desk-bound, but I do travel to visit staff about three times a month. All my staff are located quite a way from my office, so I spend a large part of my time talking to district managers on the telephone. Sometimes I deal directly with the public, usually if a complaint has reached a critical stage. I also give talks occasionally, and attend special events, such as exhibitions.

One of the high-spots of my career was going on one of the first ever exchange-visit schemes, when I spent a month in Sweden at British Telecom's expense, learning all about the Swedish telecommunications system. Although that was a fascinating trip in itself, my own day-to-day routine is rarely boring. My only regret is that, as a trained engineer, I now miss the practical involvement with all the different equipment which I used to enjoy so much.

I'm married and have two teenage children, and I'm still looking to better my career in the future, in spite of the changing face of British Telecom. I'm having a break from studies at the moment, but I hope to try for an honours degree in technology later. I dabble in local politics, do a bit of DIY around the house and relax in the winter by modelling wooden ships. I also try and work off some of that desk flab by swimming and walking!

Records and files are easily accessible.

Appendices

Jobs in British Telecom

The following list gives a rough guide to the jobs which are open to young people of different educational levels:

General secondary education
Audio, shorthand and copy typist
Catering assistant
General assistant (mainly postal duties)
Telephonist

GCE 'O' level standard(CSE grade 1)
Apprentice technician
Clerical assistant
Clerical officer
Junior drawing office assistant
Personal secretary
Trainee factory technician
Trainee technician apprentice
Data processing officer

Grades open to 'A' level holders
Commercial officer
Telecommunications officer
Senior personal secretary

British Telecom also operates a bursary scheme which is open to people with 3 'A' level passes. A number of sponsored university places are offered on Bachelor of Engineering courses, and students on this scheme are required to undertake paid employment with British Telecom during their vacations.

Management posts
Junior management posts are open to graduates and holders of HNDs or 'A' levels. Entrants join the management and professional structure according to their qualifications and specialist knowledge. There are opportunities to work in finance, personnel management, marketing, customer services, exchange management and a variety of engineering and allied functions.

Sources of further information

British Telecom produces a wide range of literature on career opportunities for young people, covering all levels of entry. For further information, contact the general manager of your local telephone area office (whose name and address will be in your telephone directory). Alternatively, write to:

The British Telecom Centre
Fourth Floor
81 Newgate Street
London
EC1A 7AG

For a fascinating insight into the past, present and future of telecommunications, visit:

The Telecom Technology Showcase
135 Queen Victoria Street
London EC4

Books to read

Alexander Graham Bell and the Conquest of Solitude by R. Bruce (Gollancz).
Careers in Telecommunications by Felicity Taylor (Kogan Page).
Communications Machines by Sam Howard (Blackwell).
Telecommunications by Michael J. Barnes (Wayland).
Telecommunications by John Stevenson (Macdonald).
The Book of Telecommunications by L. de Vries (John Murray).
The Penguin Dictionary of Telecommunications by J. Graham (Penguin).

Index